Souver...

Mrs Marvel loved shopping.
Her home was full
of knick-knacks and bric-a-brac.

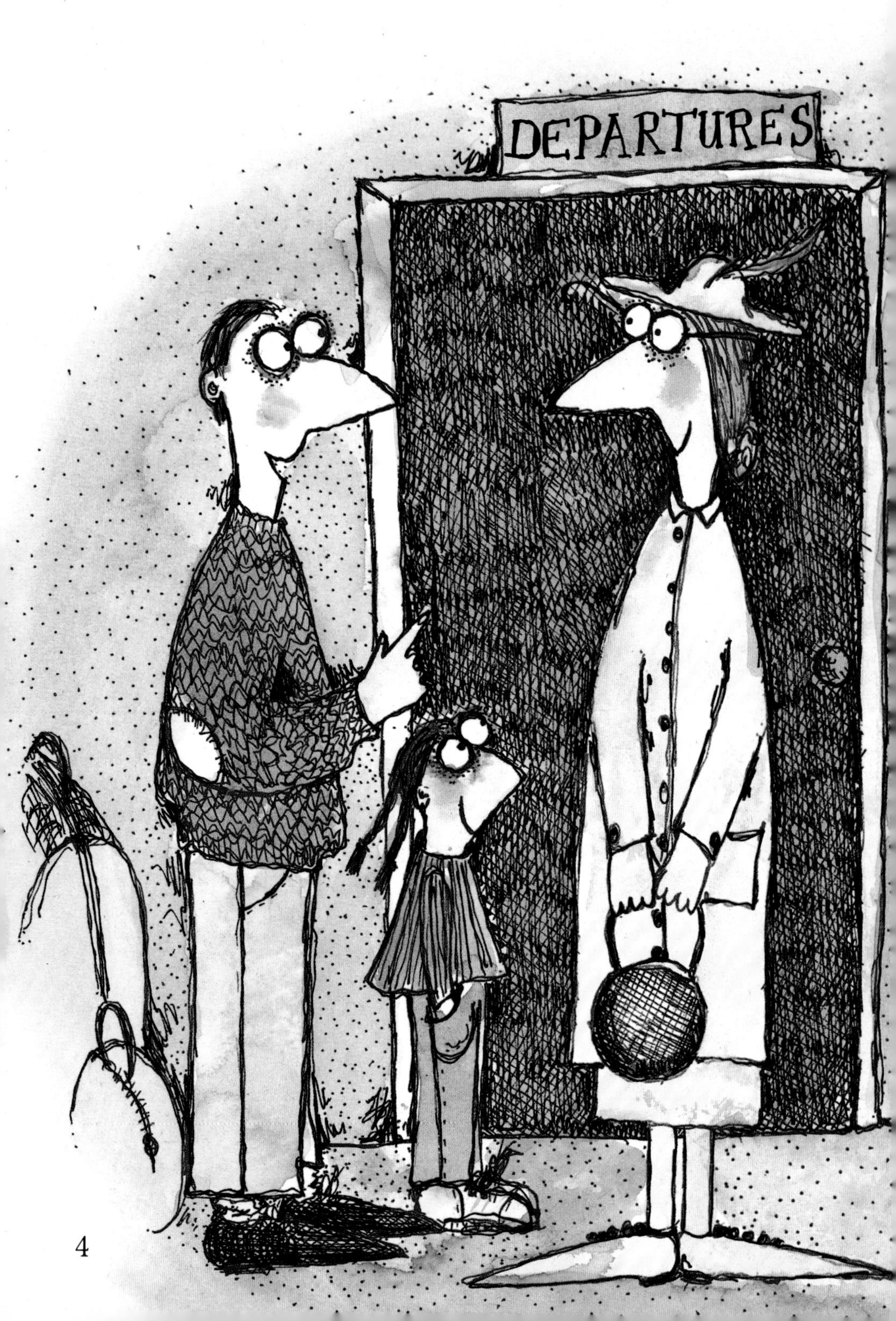
DEPARTURES

When she went on a world trip,
her family said,
"Don't buy too many souvenirs.
You will have nowhere to put them
when you get back home."

6

Mrs Marvel sent postcards to her family
from all over the world.
"The shopping is wonderful," she wrote.
"I just *had* to buy some souvenirs."
Her family shook their heads.

7

"I bought a fan in Japan,"
she wrote to her daughter.

8

"I bought a boomerang in Australia,"
she wrote to her son.

9

"I bought a surfboard in Hawaii,"
she wrote to her granddaughter.

"I bought a windmill in Holland,"
she wrote to her grandson.

"I bought a double-decker bus in England,"
she wrote to her mother.

12

Then she wrote,
"I'll be flying home soon."

"It will have to be a big plane,"
said her family.

13

14

They met her at the airport.
"Where are all your souvenirs?" they asked.

"Here," chuckled Mrs Marvel,
and she showed them...

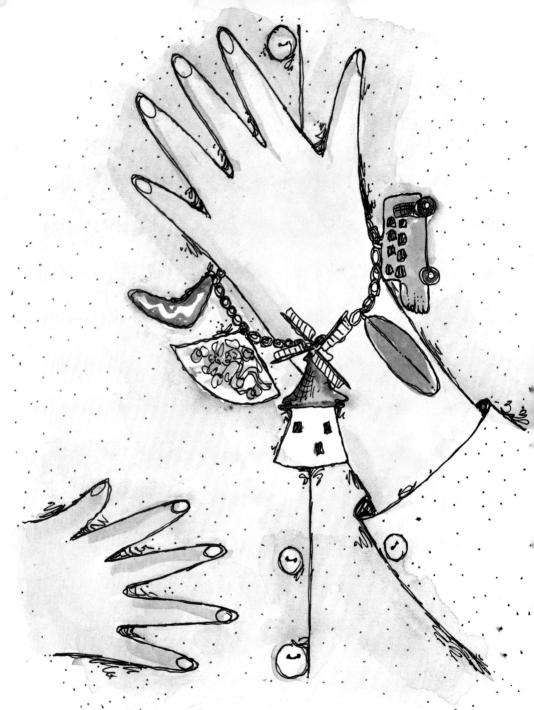

her charm bracelet.